ARE INDIAN RESERVATIONS PART OF THE US?

US HISTORY LESSONS 4TH GRADE CHILDREN'S AMERICAN HISTORY

Before the Europeans arrived in the New World, millions of Native Americans in hundreds of tribes lived all across what is now the United States. The Europeans, mainly from England, Scotland, France, and Spain, settled North America and drove the tribes out of their traditional lands. Where did the tribes go? Let's find out!

NATIVE AMERICANS VS. AMERICAN COLONISTS

WHAT IS A RESERVATION?

When the Native Americans were driven out of their traditional lands, and defeated repeatedly in wars with the colonists and then with the United States army, they lost control of what had been their country.

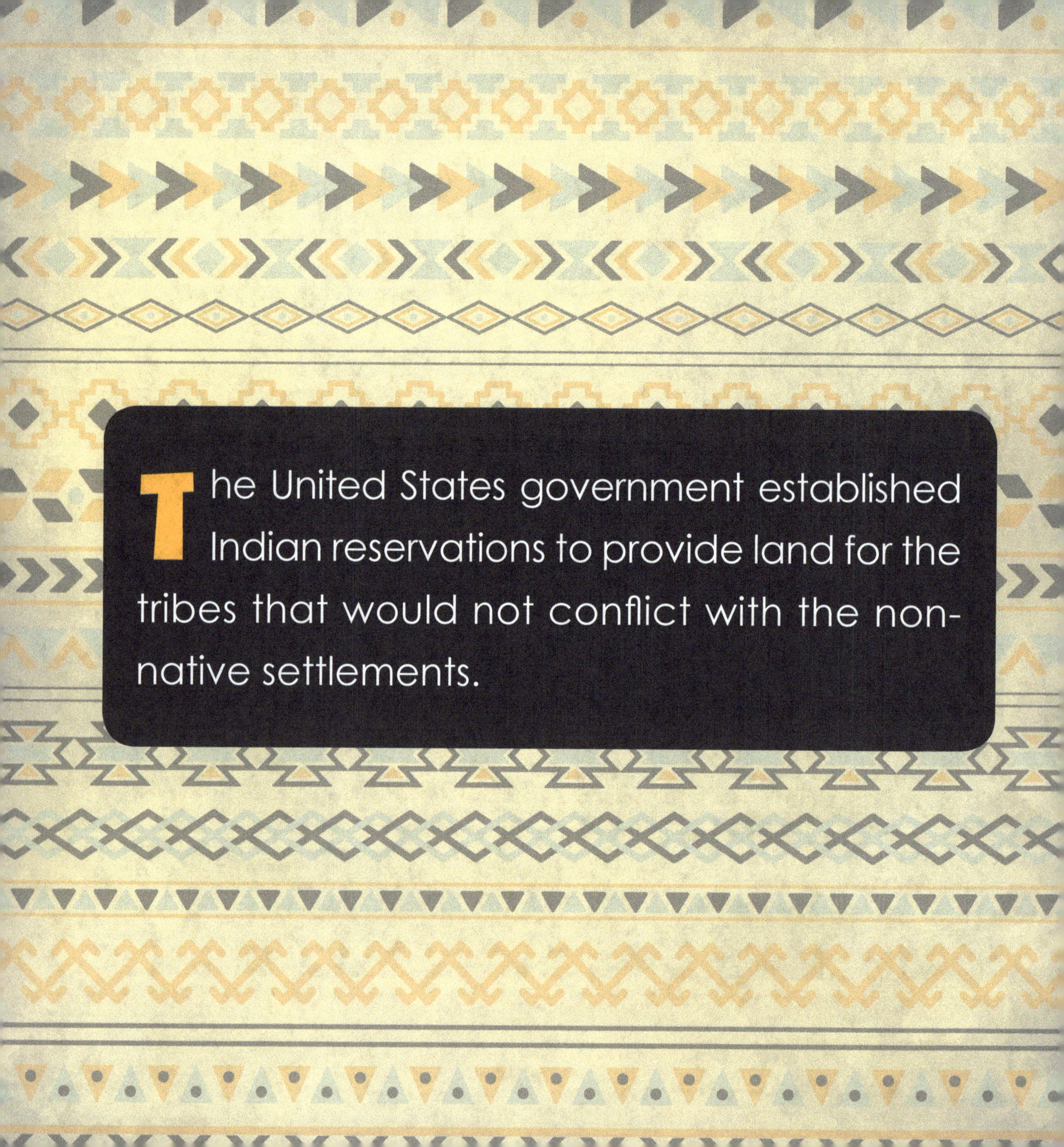

The United States government established Indian reservations to provide land for the tribes that would not conflict with the non-native settlements.

NATIVE AMERICANS ON THE RESERVATION

CATTLE GRAZING LAND

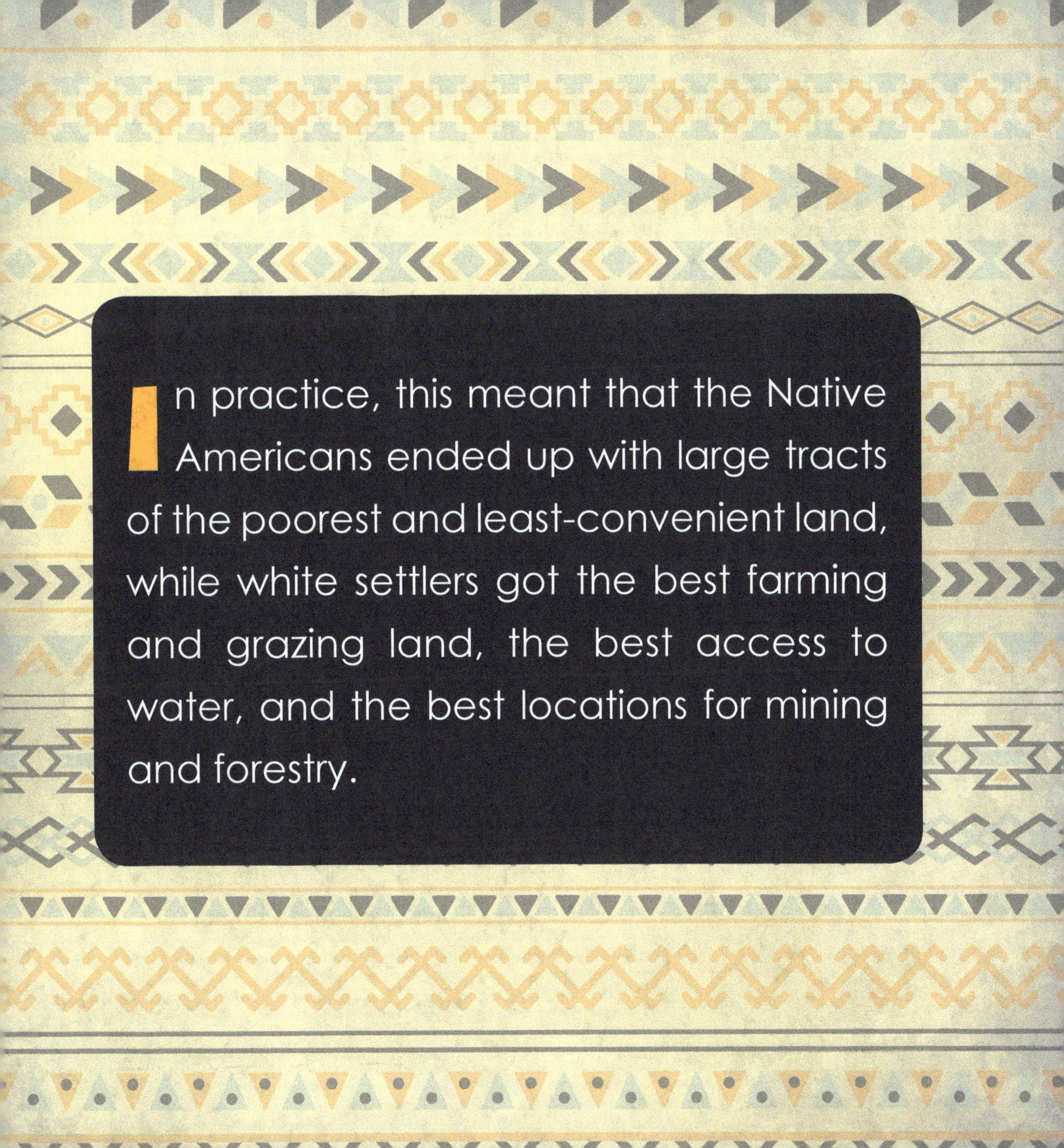

In practice, this meant that the Native Americans ended up with large tracts of the poorest and least-convenient land, while white settlers got the best farming and grazing land, the best access to water, and the best locations for mining and forestry.

O ften the tribes ended up with land far from where they had traditionally made their living. Tribes that relied on hunting buffalo and other migratory animals could no longer pursue their traditional way of life.

HUNTING BUFFALO

PEACE TREATY

A tribe gained reservation land by giving up all claims to any other land. Many tribes only did this under the threat of further attacks by the U.S. military. The reservations were often created as part of the peace treaties the U.S. government signed with tribes.

Sadly, the government often later broke the treaties when it turned out the reservation lands were more useful than the white settlers had thought. In the early 1900s some laws were put in place to better protect the rights of Native Americans and their reservations.

ARE THEY PART OF THE USA?

For day-to-day matters ranging from business licenses to local policing, from water supplies to garbage collection, local Native American governments make the rules. Tribes have their own laws, courts, and even tribal police. U.S. government laws do apply on tribal land, but state laws don't.

NATIVE AMERICAN TRIBES

In many ways reservations, and their residents, are part of the United States. Tribes can't make treaties with other countries, and reservation residents can vote in state and national elections. But in some ways tribes and the national government deal with each other as equal nations.

HOW MANY ARE THEY, AND WHERE ARE THEY?

The United States government administers over 300 land areas across the country as Indian reservations. The largest one is the Navajo Reservation, with more than 16 million acres in Utah, New Mexico, and Arizona.

NAVAJO RESERVATION

RESERVATION SETTLEMENT IN ARIZONA

Most of the reservations are much smaller, and the smallest ones are less than a hundred acres. The total land area of reservations is less than three percent of the land area of the United States.

There are reservations in 25 different states. California has the most, with over 120.

LIVING ON A RESERVATION

There are about five million Native Americans in the United States. Fewer than one quarter of them live on reservations.

The largest single benefit for Native Americans was that the reservations provided a place where they could preserve their language, rituals, and other elements of their culture, passing them on from generation to generation. Many tribes have been able to continue their existence in this way.

NATIVE AMERICANS PERFORMING RITUAL

POOR NATIVE AMERICANS

Reservations in general got land with the fewest resources and the fewest opportunities in the area. Since they start from this handicap, it is no surprise that reservation life tends to be hard. The rate of poverty is quite high, and that leads to other problems like alcohol abuse, drug addiction, and domestic violence.

Usually the tribal government and institutions like schools and federal agency offices are the largest employers on reservations. Often, working adults have to leave the reservation to find jobs, and young people who want to continue their education beyond a fairly low grade have to move to larger communities.

NATIVE AMERICANS BEING LED TO THE RESERVATION

DRINKABLE WATER

Housing on the reservations is in short supply, so many families live in over-crowded conditions, and in homes that need a lot of repairs or even replacement.

In many areas there is limited access to clean water, and waste disposal may not be up to standard. Most Americans assume they will have access to clean, drinkable water, flush toilets, reliable electricity, and of course high-speed Internet access. People on reservations can take none of these services for granted.

Some states and communities have practiced what has come to be known as "environmental racism": they have placed garbage dumps, landfill sites, and holding areas for toxic waste near to reservations so they will be as far away as possible from the homes of non-Native Americans. The residents of the reservations then suffer increased health risks from the toxic materials nearby.

GARBAGE DUMP

NATIVE AMERICAN FAMILY

HEALTH ISSUES

Native Americans living on reservations live about five years less than Americans do in general. And while they are alive, their quality of life may be much less comfortable than it is for other people in North America.

Access to basic health care, dental care, and even emergency health services can be limited on reservations, because reservation health services are systematically under-funded. Over half of Native Americans depend on the U.S. government's Indian Health Service (IHS), but the IHS can only meet a little over half of the health-care needs of the people they serve.

HEALTH CARE

PHARMACISTS AT THE PHARMACY

On reservations, there is often little access to pharmacies, preventive services such as drug and alcohol counseling, programs for diabetics or people with tuberculosis, or even people with cancer.

Here are some facts about the health situation of people on reservations:

- Heart disease is the leading cause of death.
- Native Americans are twice as likely to die of diabetes than are Americans in general.

- Native Americans are five times more likely to die from tuberculosis, and while they are alive the disease severely limits what they can do.

- Cancer rates are higher for Native Americans than for the general population, but at the same time access to programs to treat cancer, or to help cancer survivors, can be difficult or even impossible.

- Native American babies are much more likely to die before they reach three years old than are children in the country in general.

DOCTOR CHECKING THE LABORATORY RESULT OF A CANCER PATIENT

ATTITUDES

Sadly, many people in the general population hold on to attitudes about Native Americans that are far from the truth or that ignore reservation realities. This can make it harder for residents of reservations to find and hold jobs, to progress in their education, or to dream of lives and careers that might involve something different than just surviving.

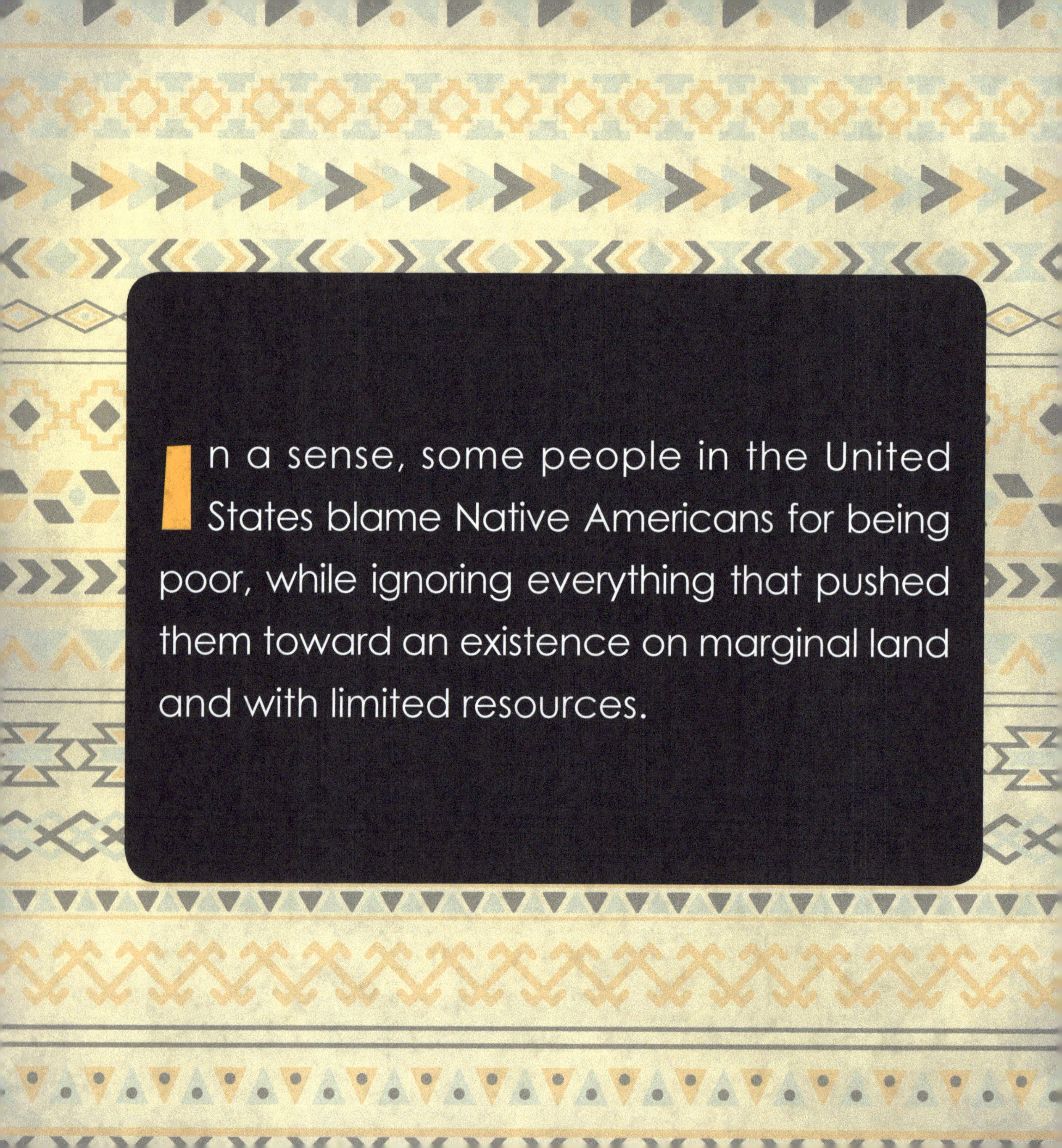

In a sense, some people in the United States blame Native Americans for being poor, while ignoring everything that pushed them toward an existence on marginal land and with limited resources.

NATIVE AMERICAN WOMAN COOKING

GAMBLING

RESERVATIONS AND CASINOS

One new feature for reservations since the 1970s is building or hosting casinos on tribal land as a way to create jobs for Native Americans and generate income for the tribe.

The first reservation gambling project was in Florida. After a long legal battle, the courts decided that states could not prevent tribes from operating casinos on their reservations, and could not tax the proceeds from those operations.

There are now over 200 casinos on tribal land, many of them owned and operated by the tribe while others are under leasing arrangements.

FLORIDA

THIS NOT
FOR ALL DEBT
Treasurer of
FEDERAL RESERVE
HC 38553744
C3
UNITED STATES
FEDERAL RESERVE
THIS NOTE IS LEGAL TENDER
FOR ALL DEBTS, PUBLIC AND PRIVATE
Treasurer of the United States.

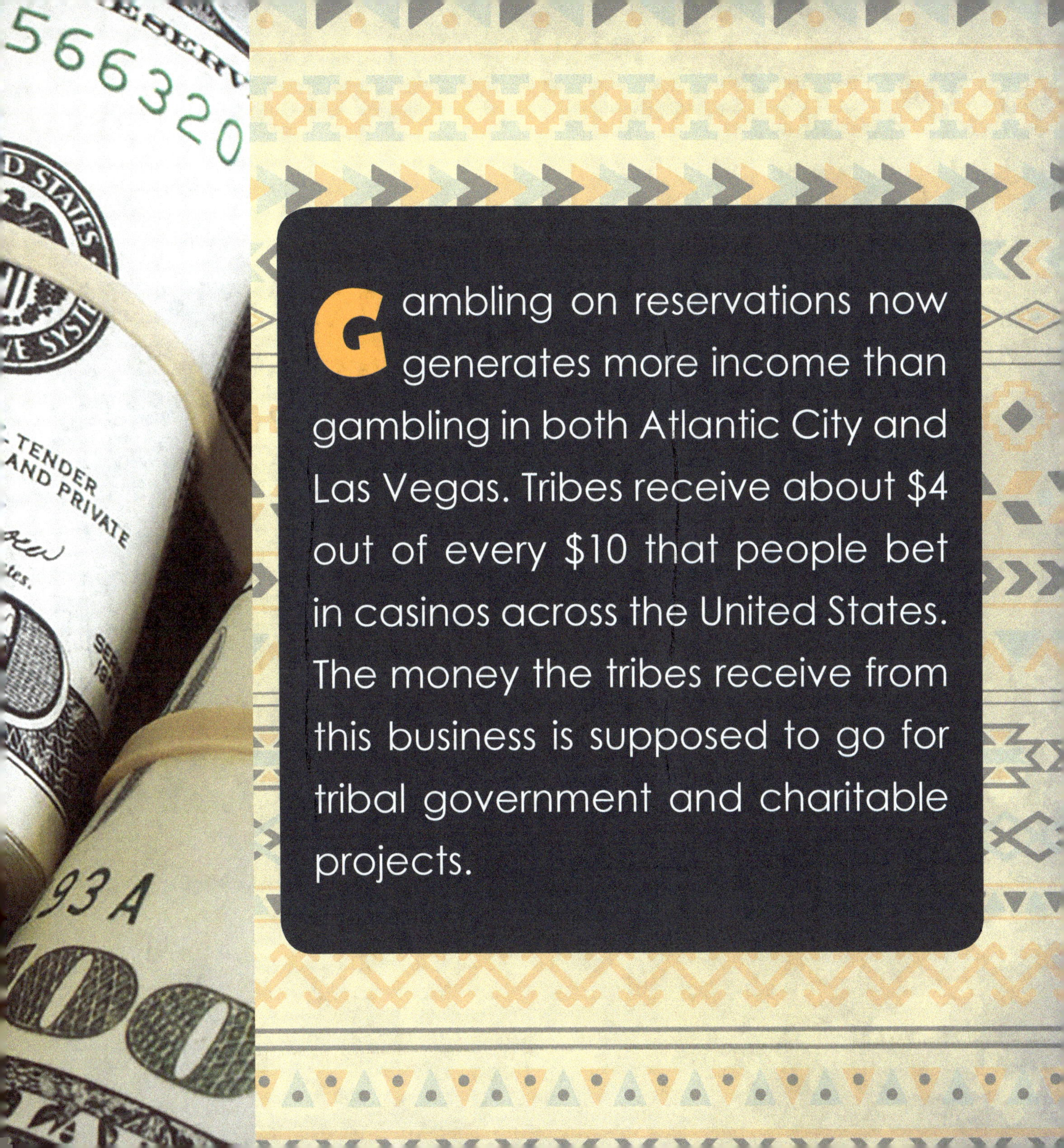

Gambling on reservations now generates more income than gambling in both Atlantic City and Las Vegas. Tribes receive about $4 out of every $10 that people bet in casinos across the United States. The money the tribes receive from this business is supposed to go for tribal government and charitable projects.

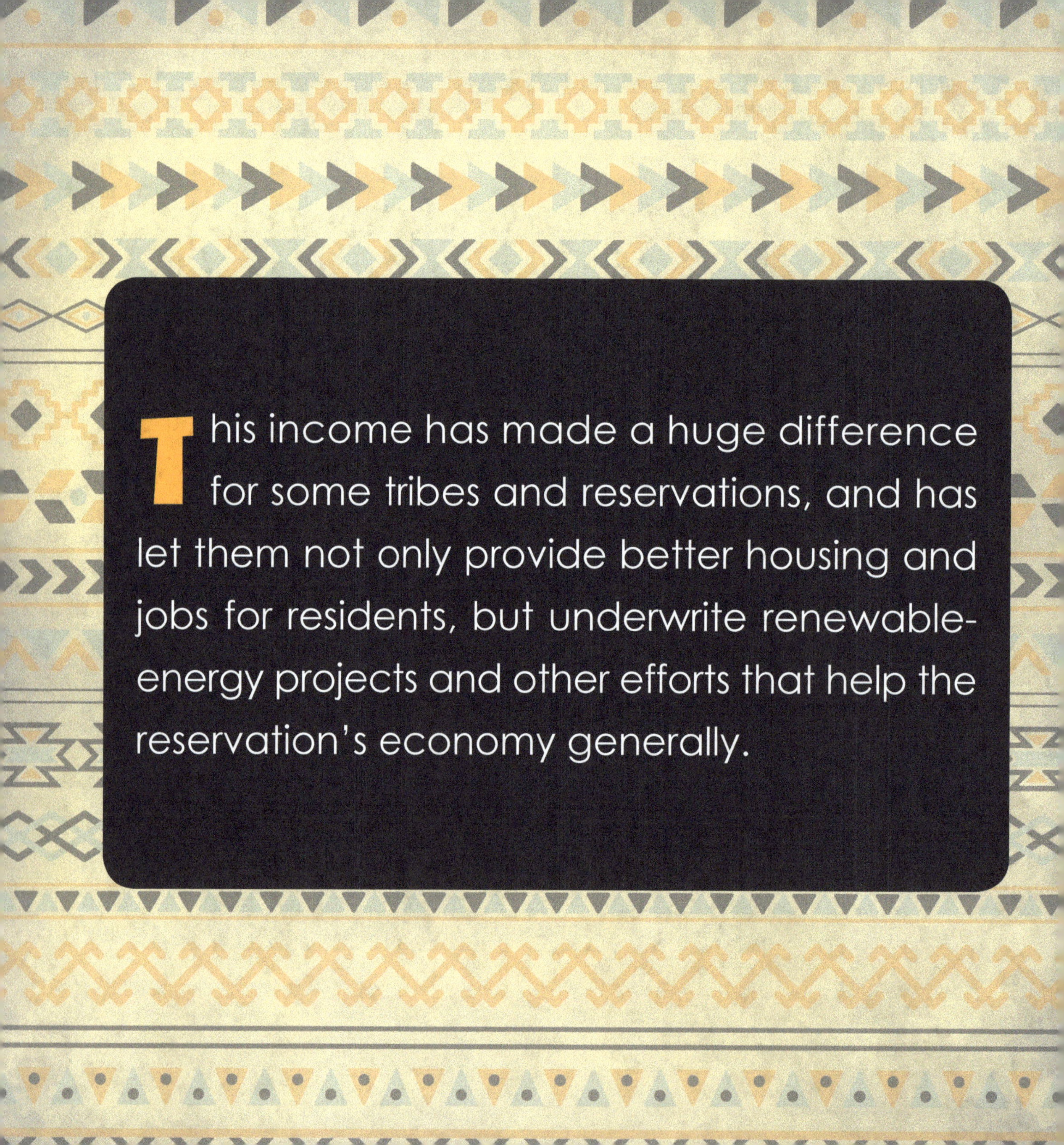

This income has made a huge difference for some tribes and reservations, and has let them not only provide better housing and jobs for residents, but underwrite renewable-energy projects and other efforts that help the reservation's economy generally.

NATIVE AMERICAN CHILDREN PLAYING
(NEW HOUSING IN BACKGROUND)

HOMELESS NATIVE AMERICANS

RESERVATION FACTS

Here are some interesting facts about Native American reservations.

- Many tribes the U.S. government recognizes do not have their own reservations.

- Over 90,000 Native American families are either homeless or living in sub-standard conditions, often on reservations. Almost half of reservation housing is considered inadequate by modern standards.

Jobs are limited in areas around reservations, and the unemployment rate for Native Americans hovers around 50 percent.

JOB INTERVIEW

- Many Native Americans work full-time but have an income below the national poverty level.
- The drop-out rate from high school for Native Americans is between 30 and 70 percent, depending on the reservation. The rate of Native Americans with college degrees is less than half that of Caucasian Americans.

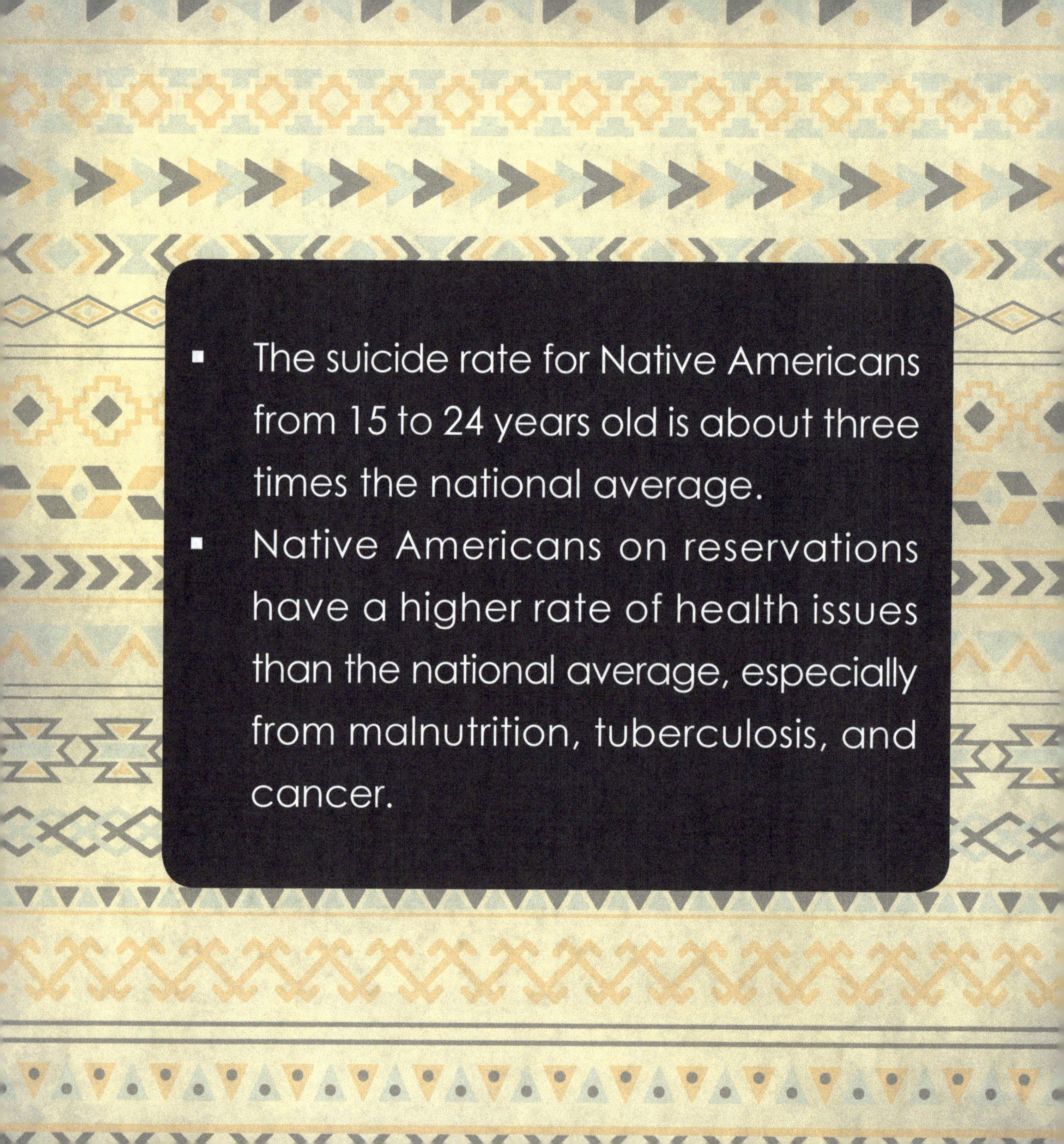

- The suicide rate for Native Americans from 15 to 24 years old is about three times the national average.
- Native Americans on reservations have a higher rate of health issues than the national average, especially from malnutrition, tuberculosis, and cancer.

MALNOURISHED CHILD

THE NATIVE AMERICAN EXPERIENCE

North American has been home to hundreds of tribes and millions of Native Americans. Once contact with Europeans started about four hundred years ago, the Native American experience changed.

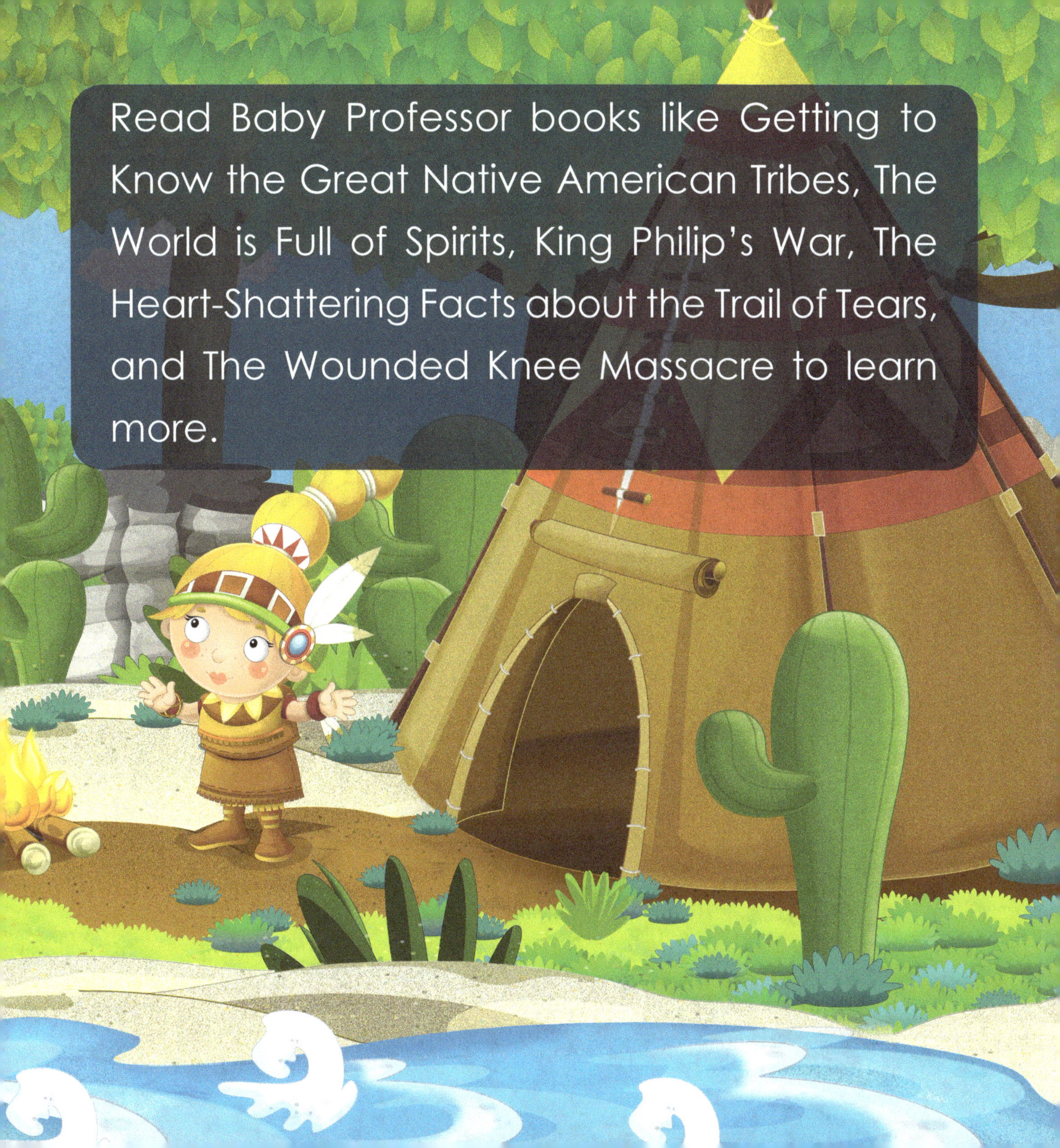

Read Baby Professor books like Getting to Know the Great Native American Tribes, The World is Full of Spirits, King Philip's War, The Heart-Shattering Facts about the Trail of Tears, and The Wounded Knee Massacre to learn more.

Visit

BABY PROFESSOR
EDUCATION KIDS

www.BabyProfessorBooks.com

to download Free Baby Professor eBooks and view
our catalog of new and exciting Children's Books